Reiki
Fur Babies

Candy Boroditsky, Ming Chee-Brown

BALBOA.
PRESS

A DIVISION OF HAY HOUSE

Balboa Press books may be ordered through booksellers or by contacting:

Balboa Press
A Division of Hay House
1663 Liberty Drive
Bloomington, IN 47403
www.balboapress.com
1-(877) 407-4847

Because of the dynamic nature of the Internet, any web addresses or
links contained in this book may have changed since publication and
may no longer be valid. The views expressed in this work are solely those
of the author and do not necessarily reflect the views of the publisher,
and the publisher hereby disclaims any responsibility for them.

ISBN: 978-1-4525-4682-7 (sc)
ISBN: 978-1-4525-4683-4 (e)
Library of Congress Control Number: 2012901919

The author of this book does not dispense medical advice or prescribe the use
of any technique as a form of treatment for physical, emotional, or medical
problems without the advice of a physician, either directly or indirectly. The
intent of the author is only to offer information of a general nature to help
you in your quest for emotional and spiritual well-being. In the event you use
any of the information in this book for yourself, which is your constitutional
right, the author and the publisher assume no responsibility for your actions.

Any people depicted in stock imagery provided by Thinkstock are models,
and such images are being used for illustrative purposes only.
Certain stock imagery © Thinkstock.

Printed in the United States of America
Balboa Press rev. date: 2/24/2012

We would like to dedicate our first written production to everyone who inspired us to tell our story; we would never have been able to share the wonders and experiences told in this book without you.

We would like to mention the Archangels with our most profound appreciation who guide us and give us strength and light to continue on this work of ours;

And all the fur babies and their caring owners who are mentioned throughout this book, you are the reason why we do this.

With gratitude to you all,
Candy and Ming

Acknowledgments

Like all creation, it begins with an idea. Once an idea begins to take shape, all of the pieces of the puzzle come together. Special recognition is given to those who provided their support and allowed us to mention their stories. It is without a doubt that when one has a vision, the Universe will bring all the right encounters, partnerships, and relationships together necessary to make it come to life. We are grateful our paths have crossed.

Arlene Mitchell, MSN

Balboa Press

Caren Myers

Carolyn Arnold
www.nurturinglifehypnotherapy.com

Jeannette Maw
www.goodvibeuniversity.com

Jon Arnold (really Carolyn the cattle prod that encouraged Jon) who pulled the words together and help tell our stories.

Lori Aldana, our friend and seamstress who turned our potato sack into a ball gown. www.iassistuoffice.com

Shannon Benecke www.holisticpetcarewithgreenz.com

Timothy Stuetz, our Reiki Master

Yvonne Kanski Horan

Introduction

"The Universe is open to all the possibilities
we dream for ourselves.
You are completely surrounded
by love, light and many angels!"
-- Reiki Fur Babies

CANDY

When I considered having my first Reiki session it was because I had not had sleep for awhile, so I was willing to try anything that would help, and it was marvelous. After that session, I did very well with sleep. For me, Reiki was better than a massage, it was better than anything I had ever experienced. It took me to the center, or core being, of who I was and I just let go. It was so relaxing. I felt that I saw lights as I relaxed, and just layers peeled away. I loved it!

MING

After doing much research, I learned that Reiki could basically heal anything. Then I thought this might be good for my dog, too. I took the steps towards learning Reiki, and Candy wanted to learn it with me. We spent some time in Vietnam practicing with using the healing energy. We returned and then learned how to do distance Reiki which we could use to do mental healings as well. During this time I was practicing on my yellow Lab, Sammy Diva, and eventually she was healed of canine hip dysplasia. This began our spiritual journey.

"When practicing Reiki, and energy healing in general, you always hear of miracles. But, when you witness them yourself, you're just always amazed."
-- Candy Boroditsky

After Sammy Diva's healing, we began to practice on people and their pets who found out about us by word of mouth. When we received their testimonials of what they had experienced, they always left us just in awe. Every testimonial still makes us stop and really take a breath in, and give thanks. There is not a healing that has happened that doesn't move us, that doesn't make us feel gratitude for what has been accomplished through Reiki and archangelic healing as well. We are very thankful that all of this happens in our lives, and your lives, and your pets' lives.

When people come to us for a Reiki session most come with the idea that they're going to be open. They are frustrated, and they come with hope that maybe this will work. One does not come to energy healing, or any alternative medicine, without hope. They don't know it's going to work, they're just open.

We bring our tools together to help with each session. We also have a lot of archangelic help – the archangels are magnificent – which makes the energy healing very, very strong. Even the animals have told us, as we started using the angels more and then the archangels came in, we asked them, "How do you feel about the energy?" They said it's even more powerful! They can actually feel themselves being surrounded by the warmth, the love, the kindness. The animals have taught us a lot about why they are here, why we are here, how they are here to help us and the connections between our souls. A lot of times we humans get attached to our diseases, and pets have shown us that they're not attached to illness. They just see themselves as souls harbored in this body, and they don't feel an attachment to it; and when it's time to let it go, they let it go. When they cross over, they have such a release, and they just depart. They don't have the baggage of us humans. They're so innocent, and so clear about what their messages are. There is so much information that they want us to know and they want us to help them get the message out, and the angels do as well. There is such an effect we all can make on the planet, together.

While healing energy has been around for centuries in the East, this type of holistic medicine, even throughout evolving time, still remains very much alive. It is notable to mention how in recent years this concept of medicine has found its way to the West, to some degree, via the rapid growth of telecommunications technology giving us the ability to research and find out about any interest through the use of the internet. We are living in a day and age where information is being shared instantaneously and we are able to make global connections at the touch of a button. Such technology has enabled us to expand our minds, interact and share ideas with like-minded people who want to learn and help spread the word about alternative medicine, including Reiki energy healing. To that end, we believe this book is a creation of a collective consciousness to find its place among those who seek healing not just for themselves, but for our beloved animals that are here to assist us with our journey. These beings have a voice not everyone can hear. It is our hope that you will find in these pages a message from them to you.

❧ 1 ❧

The Story of Reiki Fur Babies

*"Caring for the physical and mental
well-being of all creatures."*
-- Reiki Fur Babies

Candy Boroditsky, Ming Chee-Brown

CANDY'S STORY

I am a daughter, I am a mother, I am a grandmother, I am a wife, I am a sister, I am an aunt, I am a friend and I am a woman who lives in love and gratitude. I come from a poor family who worked hard and made their children work just as hard. My father was a shoe repairman like his father, and he and my mother also ran a successful restaurant in our home town of Buffalo, New York. The fact that my father had a gambling problem was the backdrop of our family life; it didn't matter how much he made he was always looking for the big score. My childhood can be recalled as very bleak with a brutal father who never spared the rod. He did love his children yet wasn't capable of knowing how to be kind. Through the difficult and miserable childhood I was able to create a wonderful life inside my mind – that's why I always knew the power of intention was real. I had to surrender the life I was living as a child because you are helpless in childhood to a higher power. We were certainly not a religious family, but somehow from within I found the strength to believe beyond my circumstances. I've always found that helping someone in need gave me the healing I needed inside me. If there's a room of a hundred people I have an internal magnet that draws me to the child or adult that has the pain I could really connect to.

When I met Ming it was because my new Boxer puppy needed to play. We moved into the same new home development and I knew no one. I scoped out the neighborhood and noticed Ming, who lived a few houses down from me, had a dog. I rang her doorbell and tried to set up a play date for our dogs. When we first met, I could feel Ming observing me. I believe it was because I say what is going on; I speak my mind, and encouraged her to try to do the same. Over time a wonderful and true friendship grew. Ming is my dearest and, for many years, my best friend. We talk and see each other almost every day. We are grateful that we have husbands who have always supported our deep abiding friendship. We certainly have had so many special adventures together. We always laugh and really allow each other the space that each of us needs just to be. I am sure that it's the comfort of our relationship that gave us the foundation to begin a business together. Ming and I are aware of each other's strengths and also our weaknesses.

My journey in this story begins with my Boxer Ry. He taught me so many incredible lessons and he introduced me to Ming. I have lived in such gratitude that God allowed Ry to live five years with so many valuable examples that my wonderful fur baby taught me. Of course I grew up with dogs and had three or four dogs before Ry. If I had to judge myself, I would say I'm a good pet owner. I gave them car rides, treats, vet visits, and above all love from all of us. When Ry came along I had an empty nest. On the same day we picked up Ry at the airport from Canada, we moved into a new house in Venice Beach. Because the house was in a new development neighborhood, the grounds were all dirt; there was no grass yet for our new puppy. The house and puppy were both brand new. Back in Pasadena while we were packing up to move, we had a big puppy shower; thirty or forty close friends came to celebrate the arrival of our Canadian Boxer puppy. It was all a fresh new beginning for us as we moved into our new home, got grass growing and started training the wildest puppy I had ever known.

Ry was so handsome, but very unpredictable. He'd be sitting on my lap so sweet, and then he would turn around and jump at my face. I would laugh hysterically because I couldn't believe this little beast! My husband and I were so in love with this guy. I brushed his teeth every morning, went for walks, and looked for other puppies to play with. How lucky for us Ming also bought a house on the same street as we did. She had a little dog called Molly. Ry and Molly became great friends as did Ming and I. Ry would talk to me over everything; he always told me what he needed. If someone called me, and Ry wanted me, he would just start howling and yelling so I couldn't hear the other person on the phone. Whatever he needed, he would communicate to me. Ry loved going to the kennel club where he played with such gusto. He would jump up and be playful with all the staff. They all fell in love with Ry, too.

Thinking back, maybe my real story began when one day when my husband and I were sitting on the couch in our living room. We were discussing my husband's upcoming surgery on a tumor that had developed on the side of his face. We were pretty confident that it would be benign. At that same moment Ry jumped on the couch and sat next to me. As I was gently petting him I felt a lump on his neck. I made a comment to my husband about the lump, asking whether he thought it could also be a tumor. I wasn't about to take any chances so I took Ry to the vet the next day to have her check out the lump. Then her announcement came that she thought it was cancerous. A needle biopsy would be done to be sure. I was stunned. I was having trouble believing her so I lived in denial until I got the results. In the meantime, my husband had his surgery. It went great. Success. It was benign. Not so for Ry. The vet called back for the follow-up visit and she confirmed her diagnosis – cancer. I called my best friend Ming because I couldn't breathe. The vet wanted me to take Ry to another veterinarian who specialized in treating dogs with cancer. The appointment was made and it was Ming who drove me and Ry to his first Oncology visit. I believe I was in shock when they called us into the examination room. I must have appeared to understand what was going on and what they were saying, but all I recall is watching their lips move in slow motion as my head tried to process their words. And then Ming and I left for an hour while they took Ry into the other room to do whatever it was they had to do. We went over to McDonald's and sat and drank diet sodas to pass an hour. Then I broke down and began to cry. It hit me right then and there. My sweet baby boy was having cancer treatment while I was sipping soda.

An hour later we headed back to the doctor, there I was in front of her again and all I could see were her lips moving. I forced myself to hear her words, but I felt too overwhelmed. The vet told us that these treatments were very expensive, they were very difficult for the dog to tolerate and they may only prolong his life by a few months. Nevertheless, I paid $1,500 and made the next appointment for Ry. Finally after what seemed like an eternity, he was brought out to us. He was very glassy-eyed and shaky, he couldn't walk without help and he had these bubbles of skin all over him. I was heartsick seeing him in such a confused and dazed state.

When we brought him home, Ming's dogs Sammy Diva and Lucy were there waiting for us. Sammy Diva licked every puffed up area on Ry's body. Each bubble was filled with liquid from his cancer treatments. It was as if the other dogs knew what he was going through and they were being so gentle and loving to Ry. Ry went back several times for more treatment, and they kept adding more drugs with each visit. As it turned out, I had to administer many of the drugs to him at home. Of course, they warned me that I must wear gloves with this medication or I could contract cancer myself. All I wanted was to do the right thing for Ry, so I was willing to take that risk in addition to spending thousands of dollars to treat his cancer.

One afternoon, on a beautiful sunny day, Ry, Lucy and I were all relaxing when all of a sudden Ry was up and running outside. I went after him and couldn't believe my eyes. Poor Ry was projectile vomiting. This lasted for fifteen or twenty minutes, then it would begin all over again. I called the vet immediately and was told that these were the side effects. After a couple of hours of this, Ry came in and collapsed on the couch. I sat with him, helplessly, and it was then that we had a serious conversation. During this conversation Ry told me he did not want to continue with the drug therapy. He had a clear voice that I could hear. My heart and head were open to this conversation. I agreed to let Ry live each day to its fullest, on his own terms. When it came to his time to pass over he would tell me. Until then he wanted to play every day, eat all his favorite foods and still go to his kennel club – he thought of it as camp! I agreed to respect him and listen with my heart. He immediately got better and started playing again like the crazy Boxer boy he always was. We were all filled with so much joy to see him living each moment with such gusto. The vet and the staff were pretty negative with our decision to discontinue chemo and all the cancer treatment, and not to mention I had a thousand more dollars worth of medication sitting on the cupboard unopened. I was told no refunds, but I could return the medication to them and they would put it to good use. Bye-bye one and all! As I write this, I'm trying to recall exactly how much longer Ry lived with us after his decision to stop the madness. I do recall though, that those six, seven months were pure magic – we lived with him in gratitude each day. He would wake up filled with promise to find the joy in each day. He ran, jumped, played ball, went to camp, ate all his favorite foods and found some new ones along the way. Ry was always jumping into the car ready to roll.

We always knew Ry's time with us would come to an end in a matter of months and so we made the decision to bring another Boxer fur baby home while Ry was still here and feeling well. My husband had heard of a black Boxer which was what he wanted. So I got on the internet and found a little black and white Boxer puppy. My husband named him Kc. The kennel club took care of picking him up at the airport and so on. Now, here were thinking we would be receiving a five, almost six month old puppy, not too young for Ry to have to deal with, but instead he looked so small, leading us to think he couldn't be more than eight or nine weeks old. Kc was also very weak and overly shy. After giving Kc a clean-up bath, we introduced him to Ry and Lucy, but little Kc was ignored by both dogs.

I had made an appointment with the veterinarian for the following day. There was, at the vet with Kc, when the vet tells me, in so many words, that our new puppy is indeed five months old, but may die. He told me to immediately drive Kc to the emergency veterinarian hospital a couple of miles away. I felt as though I was experiencing another out-of-body message with what I was hearing. Surreal. Our new little fur baby is dying! I again called my best friend Ming. She left work and drove Kc and I over to the emergency hospital for animals. I was caught up in a whirlwind of here we go again, another experience that was just too terrible to believe. When we checked in, the staff were waiting and rushed us into a room where a female veterinarian came in and examined little Kc. She told us he was very ill and may have Parvo. Next she told us that he was dehydrated along with being lethargic. She explained how they would look after him, but weren't sure that he'd live very long. As she walked out, a medical technician from the hospital came into the room and asked if we'd like to get the IV started on the dog because of the dehydration issues. Without any hesitation on my part, I replied, "Yes, please." However, before getting started, I was asked for my credit card first so that the hospital could authorize the charges prior to administering an IV on my dog. I was also informed they would be deducting $3,000 on the first credit card authorization and then run it each day that Kc was being treated. In other words, the hospital would estimate the charges daily and go "CHA-CHING!" They had me over a barrel. I had no choice, but you agree to be ransacked because you agree to the hold-up. They came back, returned my credit card and picked up Kc to take him for his treatment. They informed me that they would be in touch, although I too was welcome to phone up and check on Kc's progress. I had tears on the ride home, feeling so helpless for our new fur baby. I was greeted at home by my happy Boxer Ry and his little sister Lucy as poor Kc fought for his little life. Nevertheless, there is a happy ending to this chronicle. After this emotionally charged episode with Kc, his story spins off into him becoming our $60,000 Boxer! It's been an epic journey for him, and us, during his young life thus far.

Ry's story, however, came to an end one day after only one bad night. He woke me up at 2 a.m., pacing around in our bedroom. I got up with him. He wanted to go downstairs, and of course I followed him. He was struggling, so I held him all night on the couch. I spent that time talking things over with Ry. We agreed that he would go to the kennel club the next day and I would pick him up in the afternoon and then . . . help him pass over. My only goal was to respect him and treat him with love and dignity during the process. In the morning my husband went to work and I had an appointment to attend that day. Ming's husband Mark came by to pick up the dogs to take them to the kennel club. I left before he arrived, but I called the kennel club to alert them to Ry's imminent passing that would take place that afternoon when I picked him up. This was my gift to the staff that loved and cared for him almost five years. He also had the opportunity to say his good-byes to so many he loved in return. When I arrived later that afternoon to collect Ry, the staff was in tears. I do believe in my heart some of them were aware, as was I, that he was ready to leave his pain and struggle behind.

We drove over to the vet where they were waiting for us and took Ry and me into an examination room immediately. The vet asked me if I wanted to keep his remains. "No," I replied despondently, "all I need for Ry is in my heart. I will always have Ry in my heart, so I don't need pieces of him, thank you." As the vet listened to Ry's heart she explained that the tumors were pushing at his lungs and he was struggling to get air. Ry sat on my lap as they prepared his frail arm for an injection. I remained there with him when it was given to him. Time may have stood still at that moment because after what seemed like only a short moment, I was told, "Ry is gone." But deep inside I knew he wasn't. I told the vet solemnly, "no he hasn't, he's still here." The vet took her stethoscope up to Ry's heart and made a shocking discovery, "You're right, his heart is still beating." Then, after what appeared to be another minute or so later, I felt Ry slowly leave his body. I could feel his soul departing. With that, he was gone – on to another adventure. I moved the four-legged body of fur that had once occupied Ry's soul. Going through the motions, I got up and left the room, paid my bill, drove home and called my husband at work. He cried. I was in a cloud of disbelief, sorrow and grief, inside I was numb, but somehow I managed to send out an email notice letting everyone know Ry was no longer with us; he had passed over to begin another adventure. I also made a request that anyone who wished could make a donation to Boxer Rescue in Ry's name. Later, as I began my sleep, my tears came flooding down as the reality of his passing hit me. It was then I could finally let go and all my feelings of loss could come tumbling out. This went on each night as I would fall asleep for many, many weeks. I don't believe that grief has a time limit, but it has a course and it ran with me. Up until that day, Ry was always the wild and crazy Boxer lover boy of the kennel club. One bad day is not bad, and now I know, with all my heart, we all made the right decision with Ry and his healthcare.

I'm not certain exactly how long after Ry's passing that I began to notice I was having problems sleeping. After talking to Ming about it, she said her brother Steve had began practicing a healing modality called Reiki and asked if I would be interested in his offer to help me with some sessions for sleep. Whatever Reiki was, Steve was going to do it and I knew I could rely on his expertise to take care of me. Sure enough, my first Reiki session was absolutely wonderful, the most relaxing experience I've ever had. After just one treatment my sleeplessness disappeared. Steve offered me another session as a Christmas present. This next one was purely marvelous, even better than the first. I went deep inside of myself and uncovered many hidden issues I was not even aware of. The Reiki treatment helped me address some things I had put away that now needed my attention. It was tremendously freeing for me. Ming, in the meantime, was spending a lot of time discussing Reiki with her brother. She became increasingly interested and so she decided to study it. She made the announcement of her pursuing her interest in Reiki as we were both running errands one day and I joined her in that decision. Her brother Steve helped us find a Reiki master we could trust and in no time we were both learning Reiki. When we first met our Reiki master, Timothy, he told us we had a bright light around us. It felt a good thing as we initiated our Reiki lessons. We began our studies and eventually obtained our first degree Reiki. We proudly framed our certificates and hung them on our walls. Ming, of course was ready to learn more and I, well I came along for the journey. In looking back, I could see this is where we began on the path to study Reiki further and deeper and markedly received our second degree Reiki. We did our work with our usual commitment and enthusiasm. Upon completing our second degree Reiki we were able to go on our dream adventure to Vietnam. My husband, while he supported me fully, chose not to come along, but he did very generously give me and my best friend Ming two first class tickets and all his best wishes for a wonderful trip. (Ming and I are very fortunate because both our husbands have always been such loving and supportive men. They encourage us to follow our dreams and are the wind beneath our wings.) Our two weeks in Vietnam was an excellent opportunity for us to practice our Reiki. Wherever we went and whatever we did, I would look over and catch Ming who was Reiki-ing a fish, a dog, a child! She really did her homework and then some.

Then something else happened. After we arrived home, Ming and I went to our favorite children's bookstore, to buy some gifts for the children in our lives. While we were there reading a wonderful story about the blessings of the beasts, Ming wanted to buy some of the beautiful prints that were hanging on the bookstore's walls. Never mind that I said to her, they were very expensive. I had another idea. We would buy the book and I would mat and frame the pictures from the book. See how practical I am? They would look splendid in our Reiki office. Yes, our Reiki office! The plans and ideas were swirling around in our heads. We were now thinking of a name for our business as we were driving away from the bookstore. To this day, I still have the drawings from that conversation and the name scribbled on a piece of paper – Reiki Fur Babies. This is how it all started. We both have such a love for our animals that we always planned to take our Reiki training and use it to help the animals that bring us so much joy. And there you have it – Reiki Fur Babies was created in a car ride on our way home with our hearts filled with love for the animals in our world.

MING'S STORY

I'm from Seattle, born and raised. I like to go by the name Ming, though my name is originally Leaming, I think Ming is what I like to go by now; I'm very comfortable with it. I have two younger brothers, Steve and Peter. My parents are still in Washington and everybody is doing fine. I originally came to California to attend pharmacy school. I found it amusing as I was writing about where my journey actually began that I realized it actually starts at a very different place in my life, long before I was introduced to Reiki.

I suppose I would have to say my journey began with a painful divorce when I was faced with learning how to be on my own for the first time. It was actually very terrifying for me. I was living in a big house with a cat named Mochi, mostly holed up in my bedroom every night with my cat because I felt afraid to come downstairs and eat dinner if I was alone. Enter my best friend. As you have read throughout these pages, I had found a new friend, Candy. She was such a kind friend, nurturing me all the time, telling me to get out and survive.

In one of many conversations that took place between Candy and I, I mentioned I always wanted to have a dog, a yellow Lab. For some reason, I don't know why, I like the look of their faces – there's something about their noses that I like. So together we began searching for a dog, a yellow Lab. As it turns out, my eight year old niece, Rayne, actually took part in manifesting this desire by writing to a local Texas newspaper. Rayne wrote to Santa Claus via the newspaper that she wanted her Auntie Ming to have a dog for Christmas, and following that action, a Lab was found on the internet, exactly the age we were looking for. The moment I saw the picture of Sammy Diva I fell in love; all it took was this one picture. I learned that she lived up in a mountain in Northern California, where it was cold and rainy, and she was kept in a crate outside, along with lots of other dogs. She and the other dogs took turns going into the house, only allowed in once a month because there was an indoor cat. Sammy Diva was a retired seeing-eye-dog for the blind as well as a mother of seeing-eye-dogs. The owners had named her Diva because she had won a beauty contest, and I added the name Sammy. It so happened, Candy and her husband Gordon were heading up to that part of Northern California, near to where Sammy Diva lived, to visit Gordon's sister so they arranged to stop by and pick up this beautiful yellow Lab for me. The journey with Sammy Diva would prove to be a special journey all on its own.

On the day Sammy Diva arrived, I remember it was raining. I was at work when I got a phone call from Candy saying they were almost home. I remember leaving the office so fast I couldn't wait, I sped home. There I was in the garage anxiously waiting for her; I still had my raincoat on. Then, all I could remember next is touching Sammy for the first time, holding her ears. I didn't know Sammy had never seen a car before; she had never seen anything for that matter – a TV, stairs, anything – everything was brand new to her. When she was fed an In-N-Out burger from Candy she didn't even know how to eat it. This would prove to be a time of learning and growth for both of us.

When Candy brought Ry over the same day Sammy Diva arrived, we were under the indisputable impression they would become best friends right away. But, that was not so. Sammy was too afraid; she didn't want anyone near Candy, or near me, and Candy at last had to leave with Ry. We contacted the kennel club and told them about Sammy Diva. Their advice was to bring Sammy and Ry for a weekend so that they could bond and become best friends. We promptly acted on their suggestion and sure enough they came home after that one weekend being best friends. Ry taught Sammy how to sit for treats. It was so cute because I could still remember Ry taking his paw and pushing down on Sammy's hips. And then Sammy sat. It was an incredible thing for me to see this. It was as though Ry was saying to Sammy "this is how you get treats, you have to sit otherwise you won't get any." He taught her how to go outside where the grass was, even taught her how to eat grass if she was hungry.

As time went by, I would discover that Sammy and I had embarked on our own meaningful journey along with my cat Mochi. Together we all did very well, we learned to eat dinner – no longer was I eating popcorn. I learned to cook, and cook for myself. Along the way on this new path, I also met a wonderful man named Mark and we got married.

One day I noticed that Sammy was having trouble walking so I took her to the vet's office for a check-up and I was told her gait was off. It became so bad that in fact it got to the point where Mark had to carry her up our stairs and she was having trouble getting in our car. This is the moment when I really started thinking about Reiki, and what I had heard about Reiki being a healing energy. The true reason why I decided I wanted to learn Reiki was for Sammy. So I practiced on Sammy every day – a little bit of Reiki, a little bit of Reiki, until eventually over time she started walking without much difficulty. The next thing I know she was jumping into Candy's car! Now, when I look at Sammy's face, she reminds me of why I learned Reiki. Even dear Sammy said one day, "I wish every dog could get Reiki." So one pet at a time is our goal, giving healing to every fur baby.

As I look back to when Candy and I started out, I think how most people have a best friend, and isn't it always a dream to create something with your best friend and see it grow? It is for me, and this entire experience has been "a dream come true" for me. It has evolved into such an extraordinary journey for our friendship as well. Then there is also the joy of our friendship. One of the greatest things we have is laughter. We laugh so hard sometimes that our tummies hurt and tears stream down our faces. Humor has always been a primary ingredient of the very strong bond between us. Saying this, it doesn't mean there hasn't been any hardship faced among the two of us, but being able to find humor even during the difficult times has always been such a blessing.

To be able to recall that it was ten years ago when Candy brought her puppy to our house, introduced herself to me and my puppy, and asked if they could play together, I see how little effort it took for an amazing friendship to develop, and a sisterhood was born – the rest is history. As for me personally, Candy has always taught by example, and not only have I learned so much from her, I've come to realize over the years that we were meant to do something really big together.

There is a phrase I would say to her often and it goes something like, "Together we can do anything." I always referred this to small things here and there, but little did I know that someday something of this magnitude and this exciting was going to come out of our friendship. This phrase naturally became the basis of our company, and I continue to use it with even more conviction.

‿ 2 ⁀

What Is Reiki?

"The secret of inviting happiness
The spiritual medicine for all illness
Just for today, do not get angry,
Do not worry,
Express your thanks, be diligent in your work and
Be kind to others."
-- Mikao Usui

Reiki is an energy medicine therapy. According to CAM (Complementary and Alternative Medicine) Reiki belongs to the domain of knowledge called energy medicine. In this domain, therapies are based on the belief that disturbance of energy cause illness. So energy medicine practitioners seek to improve the flow and balance of energy in a beneficial way. The definition of Reiki as given by the NCCAN (the National Institute of Health) is "A therapy in which practitioners seek to transmit a universal energy to a person either from a distance or by placing their hands on or near the person." The intent is to heal the spirit and thus the body. Any problem involving mind, body or spirit can be benefit from Reiki. In its long history, Reiki has aided in healing virtually every known illness or injury including cancer, heart disease, AIDS, asthma, back pain, skin problems, cuts, headaches, colds, addictions and so on. In some cases people have experienced complete healing that has been confirmed by medical tests before and after Reiki treatments. Outcomes often depend on the regularity of Reiki treatments – the more Reiki you receive the better you feel. This distance healing with Reiki divine energy is used as a complement healing in almost all acute and chronic physical illnesses and ailments in children, adults and the elderly in conjunction with conventional therapy in a number of hospitals today. As a complementary healing therapy, Reiki has not only helped patients with physical ailments but also helped in relieving their stress. Reiki can be used simultaneously with other conventional therapies without any adverse effects because it is a therapy that helps to balance and align the energy you already have and adds healing to it.

We live in an age where we're surrounded by an ocean of waves – radio waves, television waves, microwaves, cellular phones, and of course computer waves. Our hairdryers, shavers and our lamps – everything has an electromagnetic wave. A hundred years ago a modern electrician would have been cast aside for claiming picture would be running wildly on a glass monitor in every living room in every home. Taking the evolution of energy and technology into consideration, as just mentioned, it should not be difficult to understand how the energy works in Reiki. Because Reiki is energy, Reiki transcends into energy healing. Our thoughts are also energy waves; they transcend time and space. Everything in our world responds to energy with people, animals and plants being the most receptive. When we send a distance Reiki treatment it's like those radio waves we talked about. Distant Reiki healing is a process of using energy, or universal energy, for healing living beings remotely. The healer acts as a conduit for the flow of energy and it's possible to transmit this energy given over any distance. Since there is no time or space in the realm, this distant healing can operate without regard to limitation of space. This is why we can send Reiki to anywhere in the world. With distant Reiki, because the animal is not disturbed, he or she can be comfortable wherever they are, and usually they just go to sleep. It's like when a person receives a great massage, they will just drift off. The animal sleeps and the energy flows where it needs to go. If it's a physical healing, that is where the flow of Reiki goes. If it's a mental healing, the Reiki heals that ailment. It is no wonder we made the decision to focus our practice on distant healing sessions, because they work so well and we've had so much success with each one.

Candy Boroditsky, Ming Chee-Brown

In the following chapter we have chosen from our library of many fascinating and remarkable stories to bring you some very special testimonies which we hope will engage you with the healing power of this wonderful, transformative therapy. It will marvel you!

❃ 3 ❧

Testimonials

"These testimonies are from the pets we've healed and the owners who love them. They are true stories and accounts of our individual as well as combined experiences with them during our sessions."
-- Reiki Fur Babies

SOPHIE ❧ Discovery of a gift!

Even though we combine our energy healing together for a more powerful Reiki session, we also have our own individual special talents and gifts that we apply, or sometimes discover, as it goes in this one encounter with a very special cat. We decided to share this story with you as experienced by each of us individually so you could be able to capture the unfolding of this remarkable account as it occurred.

CANDY

Sophie seemed so sad. I didn't know what she was being treated for, but she just seemed so blue and filled with sadness. As we connected with Sophie, I could hear a Disney tune chiming in my head, *"We are Siamese if you don't please."* And on and on it went! When the session was over, I shared it with Ming. I remember telling her how the repetition of the song playing over and over made it hard for me to focus because it kept overriding the session for me – this one song about Siamese cats. It was all so strange for me because as this tune played, I could also feel Sophie's profound sadness.

After comparing our notes, Ming decided we should share my strange experience with Mom. I let Ming do her thing, which was to provide the client with a very detailed reporting of the session, including the Disney tune episode.

MING

Candy told me what went on during Sophie's Reiki session, she had heard this cat singing a song from a Disney movie. My instant take on this was, "Awesome!" I wrote down what Candy had heard and we thought we should share it with Sophie's mom because after all it could mean something to her that we didn't know about. I put it all together in a detailed report and sent it to Sophie's mom, Caren.

Caren wrote back to us; she was in tears. "Wow!" she exclaimed. Caren recalled how this was a song she used to play for Sophie and her sister. Caren sent over a picture of both of them – two Siamese cats intertwined in playtime. Sophie was grieving the loss of Lilliana, her sister. Caren knew at that point there was no way we could've ever known any of this prior to the session. Candy and I had no idea, and it was at that moment we realized that surprisingly so,

Candy **really** can talk to the animals and hear what the animals are saying.

Candy has always been able to communicate with her own animals and because she had Boxers, she essentially thought all Boxers could talk. She didn't attribute it to herself as being able to establish communication with them on her own, she thought it was the other way around, that her Boxers were simply talking to her and she could hear them. After this session, however, there was no doubt. Now, we receive pages and pages of conversations every time we do a session with a fur baby. It's really, really terrific!

SYDNEY ❧ A Golden transformed!

This testimonial is largely significant to us as she became our poster child. She is a Golden Retriever who was a foster. When we first heard about her via email, Mom Jeannette, wrote:

"Sydney is my foster, dropped off by the Humane Society with a bunch of problems that just got worse while at the shelter. She's 40 plus pounds overweight, two infected front legs, elbows oozing pus, (the vet thought from a lifetime on cement), torn ACL in her back leg, kennel cough, matted coat that's hindered movement and she doesn't even want to move. But beyond that she seems to have lost the will to live, it was really sad. Normally when we bust a dog out of the shelter they're overwhelmed with gratitude and joy; Sydney wasn't. Not only no tail wags or smiles, she wouldn't lift her head"

Jeannette bought three sessions for Sydney and in our first session with her all we heard were sighs and feelings of pure exhaustion and no one really knew what kind of journey she had been on. We sent healing to her hips and assured her with love and healing energy. That night we heard back from Jeannette after the session, this foster Mom said she heard the clicking of nails – the Golden Retriever had actually come into the room! Then the next day the Mom sent us a picture of the dog on her back in the grass with her legs straight up in the air.

By the second Reiki session, Sydney was moving around the house and going up and down the stairs like she owned the place; she followed up thirteen steps. In the beginning foster Mom couldn't get that girl to stand up, let alone go up and down the staircase.

Then Mom told us that one Sunday morning she let Sydney go out for a potty break while she went back to bed, but the Golden followed her and lay next to the bed as Mom slept. In those few hours Mom got the most restful sleep she'd had in months. She said she woke up with a sense of peace, and that was really quite odd. Not because she was a stranger to peaceful feelings, but because she had never felt like this before. Mom said it was weird, that it was the first time she had ever felt anything like that. So she was wondering, "Did I pick up on some of this energy from Candy and Ming?" Whatever it was, she couldn't wait to do it again – "Sydney's going to sleep with me from now on!" she exclaimed.

Since these three sessions Sydney has been adopted by a doctor and is thriving and living an awesome, wonderful life.

DASHER ✎ Message of love!

This story is about a dog named Dasher. We love this story because after Candy and I sent Dasher Reiki we heard back from Dasher's Mom saying *"Oh, I forgot to tell you that Dasher's deaf, but that probably doesn't make a difference to you, does it?"* It was true, it didn't matter that he was deaf because we connected to him on a different level. Dasher had some heart problems and the first time we did a session for him there was a lot going on with him physically. When we do a session with an animal we can get the sense of their soul and there was something so sweet about Dasher. Right away Dasher said to Candy that, *"this is big, big, big"* - and he was referring to the Reiki – *"but it's not scary."* He said, *"Tell Mom no more big scary people,"* because he was at the vet and he was being poked and prodded. He told us to tell Mom, *"I'm ok, I'm not scared, but this is big, big, big."* This was really cool because he was referring to the energy we had sent to his friend Duckers, a duck!

We heard back from Mom who said she was also using the Reiki pillow we had given to Dasher and he was sleeping on it like it was a human pillow and because he is deaf, she signs language to him so he knows that she loves him and it calms him down.

The next time we did a Reiki session with him he said loudly, *"The Warriors are back for me!"* That was really inspiring, and if you want to know where the term Warrior Reiki comes from, it comes from the animals – the animals have called us the Warriors! Dasher, however, was becoming more ill, although his spirit was still strong. As we sent him another session of Reiki he said, *"Go Dasher, Go Donner, Go Blitzen!"* We were really surprised by this because we learned that is actually how he got his name, after Santa's reindeer. It was so sweet, he said he could even hear the song his dad would sing to him.

31

Dasher got very sick. On the day he crossed over, I was driving when a call from Dasher's mom, Shannon came through to tell me about Dasher's condition. I just wanted to send Dasher some Reiki and angels, and I wanted him to not be afraid. Then we cried. I told Candy that Dasher was in the Emergency Room and we should send Reiki to Dasher as he was crossing over. During that session, Dasher told Mom and dad this:

"Mom and Dad don't cry. I can feel your sadness. I'm good. I feel all the love you're surrounding me with. What a lucky pup, what a lucky pup. I'm here with my family and I'm peaceful and all my Reiki friends are here too. What a lucky pup, what a lucky pup."

The energy was so incredibly strong that Candy could sense a powerful layer of love around Dasher. It wasn't just the Reiki, it was Shannon's family! Because the love was so immense, the connection was so powerful, this love was working its effect, and Reiki is love. It was at that moment Dasher actually turned the corner and he felt a little better, even ate a bit of food. In the morning Dasher got one last session. We sent the Reiki as a cocoon to surround him, and that was just how he described it – as if he was being held in our arms. Dasher said he was glad he was home and even had his Reiki friends all around him. We later heard from Mom that Dasher had crossed over in *Dasher style*. We'll never forget Dasher. I have even asked Dasher to come visit me in my dreams, and his Mom too.

One of the most wonderful ways we can share Reiki with the animals is when they cross over, which is why this touching story makes a perfect example to share with you.

MOOSE ∽ You're never too old!

This one's got a face that I will never forget. He's just got that sweet, sweet energy that is simply unforgettable. His name is Moose. He is a 13-year-old Akita Shepherd in Denver, Colorado. When we received his Mom's email and saw his picture, our hearts were warmed instantly. We heard that Moose was thirteen plus, he had ACL surgery many years ago that healed with Reiki, he also received acupuncture, but his Mom wanted to know about distance Reiki for him. She thought she might try it for Moose, and we were very excited to send Reiki to Moose. Mom also told us there were some younger Shepherds in the house that often sandwiched him and she was always separating them, which we thought was pretty cute and funny, too.

When we connected with dear Moose, he kept saying 'oops, oops' and he was referring to himself slipping on the carpet because he was older, he felt old and there was a lot of young activity around him. Although, Moose told us he cared so much and appreciated all that his family did for him, he just was content, he was happy. He also loved the warmth of the Reiki on his hips and he loved that it flowed through him. Moose knew that it was his Mom being connected to him. After the session, we didn't hear back for a few days, but then one morning we heard from Mom. Here is what she had to share with us:

"We had a very positive session here. During the session I sat in the room with Moose and had a candle going, my husband and I meditated while the session was going on. The two Shepherds who want to be close to my husband opted to be close to Moose. I thought it was unusual that they wanted to be near him. Forty-five minutes bought such a sense of peace and calm to our usually chaotic house. It was lightly snowing outside and made it more memorable. The Reiki took a few days to set in. It's hard to notice an increase in energy because it snowed ten inches and Moose can't go on walks if the sidewalks are icy. I noticed that he did go further in the cold in the yard to do his business; his mood was also lighter. Sometimes he can be grumpy because he's aching but tonight was something else. I came home from a gig and he ran down the hall to greet me – a thirteen year old dog running! I had tears in my eyes. He was so excited and full of energy that he began barking his excited bark. What a sweetheart! Thank you for your healing work."

Candy was reminded of my own dog, Sammy, and how she was getting old yet we healed her Canine Hip Dysplasia – and now, here's this old dog running at you! There's no greater joy!

MONTY ❦ A family who Reiki's together!

We love this one because we got to Reiki not only the dog, but also the baby, the Mom and the dad. We have even done Reiki on the grandparents! So this story is about Monty, who is also one of our regulars. We just love Monty. Although Monty could receive Reiki from Mom, too, every once in awhile we would get to connect with him, and now and then Mom would say he needed more Reiki from us. There was a time Monty was receiving some Warrior Reiki sessions for pain in his shoulders and his hips; it was really enjoyable for us just to connect with him.

Monty was in Wales and afraid of the fireworks. We were trying to help him with the fireworks because he was terribly afraid of the noise. Mom said he would need Valium, but Reiki, of course, worked much better. During the session he said he had the best Mom ever and that he appreciated her looking out for him all the time. Monty said Mom was always arranging things to make sure he was taken care of. We love to hear directly from the animals that they appreciate their Moms taking care of them; it's very heart warming. Later on we got a picture of Monty completely blissed out – he didn't need a Valium! The picture said it all. Here is what Mom had to say about this session:

"Fireworks around here usually start on the weekend nearest Halloween, up to the weekend after 5th November, when we celebrate Bonfire Night in the UK. It can be two weeks of BANG BANG BANG in the evening. Of course, we can't even get home from work early to walk Monty while it's still daylight, since some people think it's fun to set off fireworks before it gets dark – seriously, what's the point of that?

I'd booked a Reiki session for Monty with Reiki Fur Babies for 5th November, as I knew that would be the height of activity around us. In the days running up to it, we had to give Monty a diazepam once or twice, but he wouldn't leave the house for walkies until morning – 24 hours of pawcrossing. On 5th, Candy & Ming were able to send him the Reiki treatment earlier in the evening just before the main displays started & with enough time to see how he'd react in case he still needed drugs. I needn't have worried, Monty was spark out asleep for most of it! The only time he got a little edgy was when Dad's parents came round with Eddie & we went out into the garden to light some sparklers. Monty tried to come out with us (I think he thought we were going to get in the car and leave him), but when we got back inside after some particularly loud bangs, he was sitting quite calmly on the sofa. Two nights before, he hadn't let me out of the house to collect Eddie without him, then he sat trembling all night, so this was a massive improvement.

Up until last week, Monty still wasn't going out after dark though. So I arranged for him to get more "Warrior" Reiki as I was away in Bremen, when I checked up on him, Dad told me he'd been waiting excitedly for walkies as soon as he'd got home from work, and has been fairly happily going out walkies since."

We were so glad that Warrior Reiki helped Monty deal with his fear of Fireworks, and no longer needed the aid of tranquilizers.

COCO ❧ Dogs just wanna have fun!

Coco is considered one of our regulars because she receives Reiki from us often. We learned that Mom rescued her from the Lange Foundation and instantly they were a perfect fit. We believe Coco took one look at Mom and that was it, they were meant to be and Mom had a new companion for life. Plus, she was Mom's very first dog! It's a true "Love Story" for sure.

Looking at adorable Coco, you wouldn't be able to distinguish Coco has pancreatitis and needs to be on a special diet. This creates a constant challenge for Mom having to find the right food and making sure Coco will eat it. She is also very allergic to fleas, causing her skin to really flare up. Coco is on the usual medications and oatmeal baths, but Mom wanted her to receive Reiki healing twice a month. Over time she has been getting better with the Reiki as well as with some other treatments.

As you know, Candy is an animal communicator and Coco was able to tell us how she felt about many things. Not every canine communicates like Coco does, but this little one makes sure to tell us what's on her mind as well as how much this little dog loves her Mama. Coco said, *"If Mama would only look into my eyes, she would see how much I love her."* She also knows that Mom loves her very much, too because she said it herself in a healing session she had in February, 2010, and told us how glad she was we were there, *"Coco is such a good girl. Mama loves her Coco. I'm glad the Reiki warriors are back because my skin is warm and itchy. Let's cool it down! Coco and Mama are very content living together. We love each other and nobody else."*

This warm and loving canine also has another side to her. We quickly learned that Coco has the funniest sense of humor and has us laughing in tears most of the time. We love her sessions because we know something hilarious is going to be said. Interestingly, we've noticed that our clients who receive Reiki on a regular basis tend to become quite comedic, and Coco, who must have been a human being in another lifetime, says things that just crack us up and tells jokes that have us rolling with laughter. Another beauty about being able to have regular Reiki sessions with our clients is that we also learn about how the energy healing works and even how the angels seem to just stay there and never leave. With Coco it's never a dull moment, Candy takes one look at the schedule, sees Coco on it and you see a smile forming on her face. Having Coco as a regular client is not only enjoyable and entertaining because she is so receptive to our healing and looks forward to our sessions, but in addition it makes our connection with her more powerful in that Reiki energy is cumulative.

During a session where we connected with Coco in August, 2011, Candy was chatting away with Coco and it wasn't until later on that she realized what Coco was talking about. The things Coco was saying to Candy had us rolling with laughter and tears streaming down our faces. Even Mom said she fell out of bed with laughter when she read this:

"You know about everything happening at Coco's end of the street. Coco always is impressed with how Coco has grown and matured over time. Mom filled our small space with 2 large people and the young, immature Coco would not have been happy with this invasion, but Coco was delighted to share with you how the time was spent. Coco is the master (actually mistress) of ceremony at Coco's home. Coco was engaging, entertaining, thoughtful and funny. Then, everyone (the two

*of them) departed and Mom went for a short drive and because of the stress and strain of our new house guests, Mom was lost. Coco means **really** lost. Mom kept driving for hours. She was trying to find Santa Barbara. Is that Santa Claus's sister? Well, because of Coco's common sense and devotion to mom, Coco stayed very quiet and still. Also, Coco thought if we got to Santa Claus's sister's house there would almost certainly be treats for Coco! It never happened. No Santa, anyone. But, Coco and Mom arrived home and just collapsed. Coco was too tired to try and help her go on line and help her to find a GPS."*

What was SO very interesting is that Coco had driven by Santa Claus Lane on her way to Santa Barbara on a day trip with Mom, and we had no idea. When we heard about this, we laughed even harder. We will never see Santa Barbara the same again!

This wise pooch has much more to share with us, though, as she communicates her feelings and wishes while she receives her healing energy proving that she really is aware and in touch with human sensory. After one of Coco's sessions in May, 2010, we had a conversation with Mom wherein she agreed with us that Coco must have been a person in a former life. She said Coco was indeed very much like a little person after she heard what Coco told us in that session: *she wanted people to adore her!* And you know what? They do. Mom takes her to see her nursing students and they fawn all over her. She also got a bath that night and sat straight up and pretty for the hair dryer just like us girls. Thinking about all this, we conclude that Coco truly believes in her core that she deserves to be treated this way – to be adored.

Well, guess what? She brings that to herself. She manifests it! She makes it so! Mom was told that Coco really can teach us all something about self esteem. Why shouldn't we be loved and adored? Coco shows us we can!

Coco also has a strong spiritual connection. A couple of sessions beforehand, we asked Coco if she could see the angels around her and she replied saying she is an angel. She went on to say that when her Mom was going through some turmoil at work, Coco was concerned but didn't know how else to help except to talk to God and Jesus! In a session from April of 2010, Coco was talking about angels and explained angels to Mom in a message that went like this:

"Mom, lesson #1 in angels, they are not solid beings, they are spiritual and can move through things. When Coco's angel is with Coco the angel is right next to, beside, and on top of Coco all at once. Mom, angels are not "real people," they come from God. Okay Mom, no, they are invisible to many people too. But, Mom, if you could clear an area, sit or lie very still with TV off, you could feel or sense the presence of the angels, or with a blessing you could hear the angel speak."

Coco has maintained an open connection with her angel over time, but still remains the comedienne canine that she is. You will really enjoy this next story that came up when, in another wellness check-up for Coco in August, 2011, we worked on her pancreas and allergies while she shared with us her pearls of wisdom:

"Coco's and Coco's angel ambassador have been in a state of grace for weeks. Of course, Coco's angel is always in an angelic state, but

everyone knows this is a new territory for Coco. Things have been very peaceful at home with Mom. Maybe this calm is spreading and everyone will contract this "disease" of peace and well being. Now with all that said, Coco would like to let the cell phone saga unfold for you. Mom misplaces, loses, and can't find her cell phone. Coco is observing Mom searching for her buried treasure all over Coco's and her Mom's home, with no luck. Yes, Coco is realizing Mom believes that Coco knows where that annoying piece of technology is, but, no, Coco does not. Coco knows a search party of ten could come into Mom's home and never find the phone let alone [their way out again].These problems occur because Mom lives on another plane where things must find their own storage solutions and places to reside with Mom's four walls. Of course, this presents many challenges for Mom, but Mom also has had many surprises, too. The surprises come whenever something turns up that Mom thought was lost or gone forever, or Mom doesn't remember losing it in the first place. Please don't stress out about these minor occurrences because Coco doesn't. Relax, and have a dish of ice cream."

Mom told us after the session that Coco was getting some tiny scoops of yogurt or ice cream, which explains her last statement in that conversation. "Relax, and have a bowl of ice cream!" She not only makes us laugh, but does teach us – What *if* we all caught the "disease" of peace and well being?

Throughout our monthly sessions of Reiki Energy healing for Coco over the last year-and-a-half, we have sent her physical healing for her pancreas and all her internal organs, shielded her from fleas and ticks by coating her body with Reiki much like it's a balm to keep her allergies at bay, balanced her chakras, and have even seen the angels petting Coco and scratching her. Mom has told us about concerns she has had with Coco and boundaries, and sometimes Mom has become frustrated with her, other times Mom just wants to make sure Coco isn't feeling lonely while she's away. We have communicated with Coco to comfort her and ease her mind. She has reminded us that, *"Coco was raised in a chain gang where dog ate dog; survival of the fittest. All that hard core stuff. Coco is really trying to readjust to life with a kind and loving Mom. Coco keeps doing Coco's best."* We could all learn a little something from this incredibly sweet, loving dog. Even though she has come from a rough background where not a lot of love and affection was given to her, she still has a big warm heart full of love to share with Mom and anyone else who needs comfort. Moreover, she accepts the healing energy of Reiki and the angels with appreciation and anticipation, while keeping them always by her side.

We were told by Mom after one of Coco's sessions that she was so blissed-out, her head was just hanging off the couch. Mom carried her to bed and she slept soundly the entire night! We look forward to connecting with Coco again very soon! And we will.

TINKERBELL ✎ Miracles are real!

We met Tinkerbell last year after meeting Mom at a conference where we introduced her to Reiki and, of course, us – Reiki Fur Babies. A few months later we learned she had a 12-year-old Bichon named Tinkerbell, so we decided to give her a blast of Reiki for overall wellness. This would also be the first time Mom and the family had encountered energy of this nature, a discovery beyond anything they had ever known existed and that left everyone in amazement. This is because Tinkerbell's story involves an experience that some may very well call a "miracle."

Tinkerbell's first session was a rather interesting and comical meeting as she greeted us in a foreign language and she revealed that she was actually trilingual.

As we connected with Tinkerbell, first thing she said was "Como Sayama." Candy and I both don't speak Spanish, but we told her who we are and that we were going to send her some healing energy. We told her our names are Candy and Ming. Tinkerbell said her name is Tinks. Tinks said, "Tinks can speak Spanish, English and Doglish. Whatever is needed for Tinks to be heard?" Ok, English it is! Tinks sees all the angels and they have told Tinks that they were here because Tinks is so loved and special. Tinks always feels loved and Tinks does like all the calming gentle way each angel came to see Tinks. Each Archangel took the time to go to Tinks, pet Tinks and send healing energy to Tinks. Tinks does like this. Tinks says sweet just like Tinks. "Healing energy flowing through Tinks' precious body sounds so wonderful," Tinks says. Tinks does like to be in charge so Tinks is very happy with the information that Tinks can have this healing energy work on Tinks' "command"! Tinks was told that Tinks can ask the angels to help her at anytime. Tinks is really having "party" right now in her body. Tinks said, "Tinks' Reiki party!" Tinks' body is celebrating and Tinks says, "Thank you, mucho gracias."

Tinks was so funny. We sent the healing energy from her head to her tail, all of her organs, heart, lung and her hips, spine and muscle. We gave her a good wellness check up. This energy will flow for awhile depending on how she needs it. This was the first time we heard a fur baby call it a "party"…very cute!!

Mom said she could feel a warmth in the room while the session was taking place and Tinkerbell, who shared space outdoors with her buddy Amber, was perking her ears up and looking around, until she finally cuddled up to Amber and dozed off. She shared this with us as well:

Amazing report!! My daughter & I thought i[t] was so funny about her Spanish inquiry. You know she spent a few years living w/ my mom, so it's no surprise she knows Spanish. At one point my mom said she had transformed her into a Spanish speaking dog haha, maybe that's why she barks at us so much, she wants to speak Spanish LOL. She looks happy, and Ashlen

says "she gives a whole new meaning to being a 'party animal'."
Wonderful stuff, thank you again and again!!

Two weeks later, Tinkerbell's buddy Amber, a 10-year old German Shepherd, suddenly passed, and the family was grief-stricken with such an unexpected loss. Tinkerbell was then transferred inside the home so she wouldn't be alone. She was going through abrupt changes – missing Amber, being relocated indoors from her outdoor environment – all at once things became different for her, and we explained to Mom how she needed reassurance as she instinctively picked up on how everyone in the home was feeling and that she would be dealing with this loss in her own way because animals grieve, too.

In regular communications with Mom, we were kept up to date on Tinkerbell. All was seemingly fine until one night a text message came through from Mom, apparently distressed because they had just learned that Tinkerbell had tumors on her chest which the vet diagnosed as most likely being malignant. He told them that she was beyond anything he could do for her and she would need to be put to rest. She was brought home for the family to say their good-byes and in the morning she would be taken back to the vet to be euthanized if she even made it through the night. As everyone cried and struggled with the news, Mom asked us to connect with Tinkerbell to let her know they just wanted what was best, and how much they loved her so. When Mom sent us a picture of Tinkerbell's sad little face, we told her we would cheer her up and reminded her that the last time we connected with Tinks she was very strong hearted and saw the angels. Later that night, we reported this back to Mom:

As we connected with Tinkerbell, Tinkerbell said, "Tinks is very sleepy and just feels worn out today. Everyone except the angels is sad around here. Tinks can't comfort the family so maybe Tinks can share this healing energy with ALL of them. Tinks knows that Tinks is sick but Tinks does not feel the sadness about this. Tinks believes that this is Tinks' journey and Tinks knows that it's all going to be grand. Remember, Tinkerbell has angels with Tinkerbell all the time. These angels really keep Tinkerbell feeling all the love there is for Tinkerbell. Tinks knows her family is taking the best care of Tinks. Tinkerbell is loved by so many kind and loving family members. Tinks will ALWAYS stay connected to each of them. Tinks is not just a ball of fur, but Tinks has a soul that will always be with ALL of my family. Please let them know that Tinks feels their love and pain. Tinks is at peace and knows it will be okay."

Tinkerbell is tired, she does not appear to be in pain. She will be connected to each of you always and forever. What she shared about having a soul is so sweet. Her journey will teach all of us how strong our connections are with our fur babies.

The angels and Archangels are with her, they will always stay with her. They have been with her. They are comforting her. There were also many spirit animals around her giving her healing as well. Saw a horse, some cats, they were all assisting.

We sent healing to her physical body to give her comfort and peace. Also, to shrink the tumors if at all possible. Tinkerbell is right, this is her journey.

Forty minutes later, we received an email from Mom. The excitement and amazement came through in her email:

"She is up, walked, and is now on the sofa w/Bob & Ashlen. She is still in some pain & discomfort, but Wow, we have witnessed a miracle. If she is like this through the night & is perky in the morning, we will just let her life take its course. Thank you, thank you, I just can't thank you enough! Love & Blessings."

That night, Tinkerbell ate a little food; the next day she sunbathed outside with Mom, while Mom prayed and asked the Archangels to heal Tinkerbell. By the next evening, she was a bit more lively and eating again. When we checked up on her a few days later, Mom said, "Tinkerbell had a great weekend. She has been given a second chance at life and she's enjoying every minute of it. I hope her tumors will "relax", if not completely go into remission, so she can be pain free and just be Tinks for as long as possible." We agreed to give her two more healing sessions in the following weeks.

Second Session:

As we connected with Tinkerbell, Tinkerbell said, "Tinkerbell feels you and feels the healing energy. Tinkerbell feels the love surrounding Tinkerbell all the time. Tinkerbell never feels sad because of all the angels and Tinkerbell's family loving and protecting Tinks. Tinks rests a lot and absorbs all the kindness coming in Tinkerbell's direction. Tinkerbell feels so calm and peaceful from within. Tinkerbell knows that Tinkerbell's connections with Tink's people will last a lifetime. Tinkerbell is really grateful for all the love and blessings that Tinkerbell is showered with daily."

We sent physical healing all through Tinkerbell's body directing the healing to the tumors in her chest shrinking them so they do not grow or press on any organs. We also balanced all of Tinkerbell's chakras. All of the angels are there with Tinkerbell. We asked Archangel Raphael to continue to heal Tinkerbell as well.

Keep us posted on Tinkerbell! She is living a life of gratitude!

Third Session:

As we connected with Tinkerbell, Tinkerbell said – "Tinkerbell likes when you arrive here for a healing visit. All the energy in Tinks' home becomes more powerful. Tinks can really feel the vibration of this healing energy. Tinkerbell feels the wave lengths of energy and then Tinks directs them inside Tinks body to heal Tinks. Tinkerbell wants to help everyone who is helping Tinkerbell. Tinkerbell knows the whole family is getting to absorb this healing energy. Tinks is really feeling good with life. Tinks knows that Tinks is being cared for all the time. Tinkerbell has people and angels loving and protecting Tinkerbell. Tinkerbell will just relax, rest and let life be."

When Tinkerbell speaks of participating in her own healing, she is talking about her wellness center. Healing energy activates that wellness center as spoken in one of our blog posts.

Tinkerbell, because she has had more than one session, has learned how to move the energy to where she needs it... this is why it's important to have cumulative sessions. It's so awesome Tinks is so intuitive.

Archangel Raphael assisted us in shrinking the tumors! Let us know how she does!

Mom truly believes they witnessed a miracle. At the end of that same month when Tinkerbell had been recommended by the vet to undergo euthanasia, Mom told us in her own words, *"Tinkerbell is doing wonderful - no more inflammation, she runs around like a brand new fur baby :D I don't think she could've survived without the Reiki you and Candy sent her. And I am just so happy I found you ladies!"*

Could Reiki produce miracles such as this one? If one is open to miracles, and if the journey we are on consists of being witness to such miracles in order to help us along, yes – it is a balance of Reiki healing energy, love and an open heart. Tinkerbell's journey is not over. She still has some life left to continue to teach us. She opened herself up to us and the angels, and let her illness take its course which ultimately led to the healing of her tumors.

∞ 4 ∞

Animal Soul Connections

"Until one has loved an animal,
part of their soul remains unawakened."
-- Reiki Fur Babies

Throughout our experience as Reiki healers for fur babies and in speaking with pet owners, we have discovered that human beings and their pets can actually form a soul bond. Perhaps you had a dog that was your best friend and companion, or a cat that felt like one of your children. When a person feels highly connected with their pet it is probably because of something that was formed way back in time, in a past life if you will. The soul of that animal develops a strong bond with our soul and many times that soul can return as another animal or a similar one. For instance, you may experience that the dog you have now has similar characteristics as your previous dog. Whether we materialize our pets in this life or whether they come back to us by their own free will, we believe that our beloved pets have their journeys to live just as we do. However, their journeys are different to ours in that they are here to teach us about gratitude, peace, about not being so attached to our surroundings, and more over about LOVE. How do we know this? All animals are able to communicate with human beings and anyone is able to tap into any animal that is open to share with us if we too open up to them.

We are all born with the capability of communicating with our fur babies and they definitely know when we are happy, sad and even ill. They love us so much, unconditionally, that pets will even take on our diseases to help assist us. Candy experienced this type of transference with her husband and her beloved Ry. Remember the story Candy shared in Chapter 1 when she talked about losing her five-year old Boxer, Ry? Candy's husband had developed a tumor on his face. A few days later, she discovered their dog Ry had a tumor as well. While Candy's husband's tumor was benign, Ry's tumor became malignant and ultimately ended his precious life. We do believe that Ry came back as a female Boxer named Star. For this reason, we always encourage our clients to try and stay in balance, if not for their own sake, but for their pets.

Animals have highly acute senses that enable non verbal communication not only with human beings, but amongst their own members as well as with other species. They have a language just like we do which is why thousands of birds can flock together. Even those animals who fall into stereotypes such as cats and dogs that supposedly dislike each other, though they may not care for each other's personalities, many of them actually love each other to the point where they can even sleep next to one another. They are communicating! An elephant once told us she learned she could communicate with all the other elephants without "speaking" aloud.

Just as there are bonds we form with living animals, there are also connections we form with animal totems or spirit animals. They are bringing us messages be it in a dream or they will appear to us in meditation, sometimes we will keep seeing them in waking life while driving, walking, or just out of the blue. For instance, if a hawk should appear to us it usually means there is a vision coming. Animal spirit guides may come at different times in our life depending on where we are in our own journey. These guides are here to give us guidance and support. There are different people who can assist with finding out who your animal spirit guide is and you may even discover you have several.

It is important to remember that when the journey comes to an end for our animals here on earth, they continue to look after us from the spirit world. Someone once asked us if all dogs and cats go to heaven. Heaven is a personal place for every being, but we do know that all animals cross over to another realm where they are happy and are without pain. Many of them enjoy it there because they are able to assist us humans better from where they are, and some even have a Reiki practice of their own. Imagine if you could see a cat stretching its paws out and sending healing. It's quite a sight! Whether or not this place is called "heaven" only they know, but it is certainly a peaceful and happy place!

Conclusion

*"Nature is full of amazing & wonderful things;
we have so much to learn from nature's
animals, if we do listen!"*
-- Reiki Fur Babies

CANDY

It begins again. I'm at the sink washing dishes after a lovely lunch on Mother's Day, no less. Star and Kc are yapping, barking and going crazy! I choose to ignore it, until I could no longer take it. I put the dishes down and march straight out to the garden where I witness Star had bent the fence half way down and was still barking like a lunatic. Sure enough, it was that darn squirrel – back again tormenting my Boxer babies! I looked around the yard, scanning the area to see where this rodent was actually at. At first glance I failed to locate him, so I made my way to the half-falling fence to try and straighten it back up. All of a sudden, my gaze turns just 2 feet away from where I was standing, and from a nearby branch in my orchid tree I hear this "gibberish." It is not the usual piercing sound of a squirrel's squeaks; instead I hear a conversational gibberish. I'm stunned! Of course, by then I'm instinctively looking for a rock, but to my utter astonishment the squirrel has me in an irresistible hold as he put up a paw and began to talk to me. I slowly brought my arms down to my sides as we made eye contact and Squirrel continued to talk. By now he is chit chatting away – I am mystified. Here I am observing him as his eyes are glaring and fixated with mine, one paw up – at times both paws up, saying, "Please pay attention to me!" I could understand everything he was saying. It's like when you meet someone from a foreign country and they are trying to tell you something, but you don't speak the same language yet you are still able to communicate? I'm sure this has happened to most of us at least once in our lives, albeit, this is the first time a rodent and I have ever connected in conversation. How could this be happening? I know it happens to people with their pets…we all communicate with our pets, but this is not my pet, this is a rodent that has been annoying me for months!

Something strange happened to me – I started to talk back. I found myself asking him how he liked the reiki. He told me that's why he was talking to me. Next thing I know, he's chattering to me that if I was willing to reiki him, he was willing to talk to me. And there he had me. It was at this moment I was reminded about a book that Ming and I had read together years ago entitled "The Blessings of the Beasts." This book is about a skunk and a roach telling a tale about their journey to be blessed by St. Francis. This encounter was a reminder to me that Squirrel was every bit as important as my dogs were to me. After all, this squirrel was telling me he, too, *is* a fur baby. Our intuitive conversation went on for almost 30 minutes as he moved around trying to get closer to me. My Boxers were standing in back of me the whole time after telling them to quiet down; they too became mesmerized by the chatty squirrel talking to me. Even my neighbour who was in his yard next to me came over the fence and whispered to me, "Is that squirrel talking to you?" I made no response. My focus was entirely on my new lovely rodent friend, the squirrel.

I have to say, what a transformation I experienced. It was thirty minutes of an awakening in my own garden by a squirrel. It just shows you, you never know who or what will move you. On that particular day, for me, it was one little inciting squirrel that stirred up something inside of me and moved me to tears making me realize that **all** of God's creatures are precious and do indeed have value.